Now Cow Helps Lost My Shoe Caribou

A Mindful Tale for Personal Responsibility

by Kelly Caleb
Illustrations by John Van Hout III

Visit our website at NowCowBooks.com

Facebook.com/pg/Now-Cow-Books-Inc-101688601393826/
instagram.com/nowcowdramallama/
twitter.com/nowcowdramalla1

Copyright 2020 © Oldsmar, FL Now Cow Books, Inc.
All Rights Reserved

No part of this book may be reproduced or transmitted in any form or by any means, electronic or mechanical, including photocopying, recording, or by any information storage and retrieval system without permission in writing from Now Cow Books, Inc.

Library of Congress Control Number: 2020915737
ISBN: 978-1-7333783-6-9
Now Cow Helps Lost My Shoe Caribou: A Mindful Tale for Personal Responsibility
Kelly Caleb
Illustrations by John VanHout III
1st Edition, Book 3 of the Now Cow Series
Book 1 - Now Cow Helps Drama Llama: A Mindful Tale for Coping with Anxiety
Book 2 - Now Cow Helps Bad Habit Rabbit: A Mindful Tale for Changing Behaviors

Dedicated with love to the following amazing people:
My son David and his wife Ashley
My daughter Tiara

Unending Thanks and Appreciation to
Liz and Paul Martin - who keep me moving in the right direction.
Dawn Barach - who inspires me with her creative sewing and generosity of heart
Serrena Blaize - who has kept me sane and moving in positive ever expanding levels of creativity and writing when I was channeling my inner lost my shoe caribou!

Always and Forever:
To honor the memory of Jack Cole Martin and assist children and adolescents with the challenges of mental health (and particularly to fight against issues of bullying and suicide by educating and promoting acceptance, belonging, and positive actions that lead to good choices), 10% of all profits from the Now Cow Book series are donated to operationjacksvillage at https://operationjacksvillage.org/.
#operationjacksvillage
#istandwithjack
#HOPEInnovators

Lost My Shoe Caribou
lost a lot of stuff

And when he could not find
his things, he'd end up in a huff.

He'd try to find it here and there with very little luck

And then he'd say, "It's not my fault" and try to pass the buck.

He'd ask his friends, "Have you seen this - my blue and green striped hat?"

"I had it only yesterday. I lost it after that".

His friends would join him in the hunt.
The largest beast,
the smallest
runt.

Sometimes they would find his thing
- A hat, a shoe, a truck...
When he lost it yet again he'd say,
"I guess that's just my luck"

One calm friend watched this
go on and on and on and on

Now Cow spoke up "Dear
caribou, forgive the intrusion,
But I feel it's time to say responsibility

Is something you are lacking,
and alas, I fear it's key.

Let's take
some time to think
upon this with serenity
For even caribous must
have accountability."

The caribou protested,
"Now Cow, it's not my fault.
But if you think that you
can really bring this to
a halt,

This losing, searching, finding trend
I really do wish it would end

I surely want these things to change
My whole life to rearrange

But I can see no end in sight
It seems an endless losing fight".

"Take heart, my friend" Now Cow replied.
"For objects know not how to hide.

We simply need your steps to trace.
And know that this is not a race."

And while we walk, we'll meditate,
Breathe in and hold. Count to eight.

And then breathe out slow and sure
To make our hearts and minds more pure".

"Breathe in and out?
Why? Is that new?"

"It gives your mind something to do
To keep it focused laser straight
A simple way to meditate"

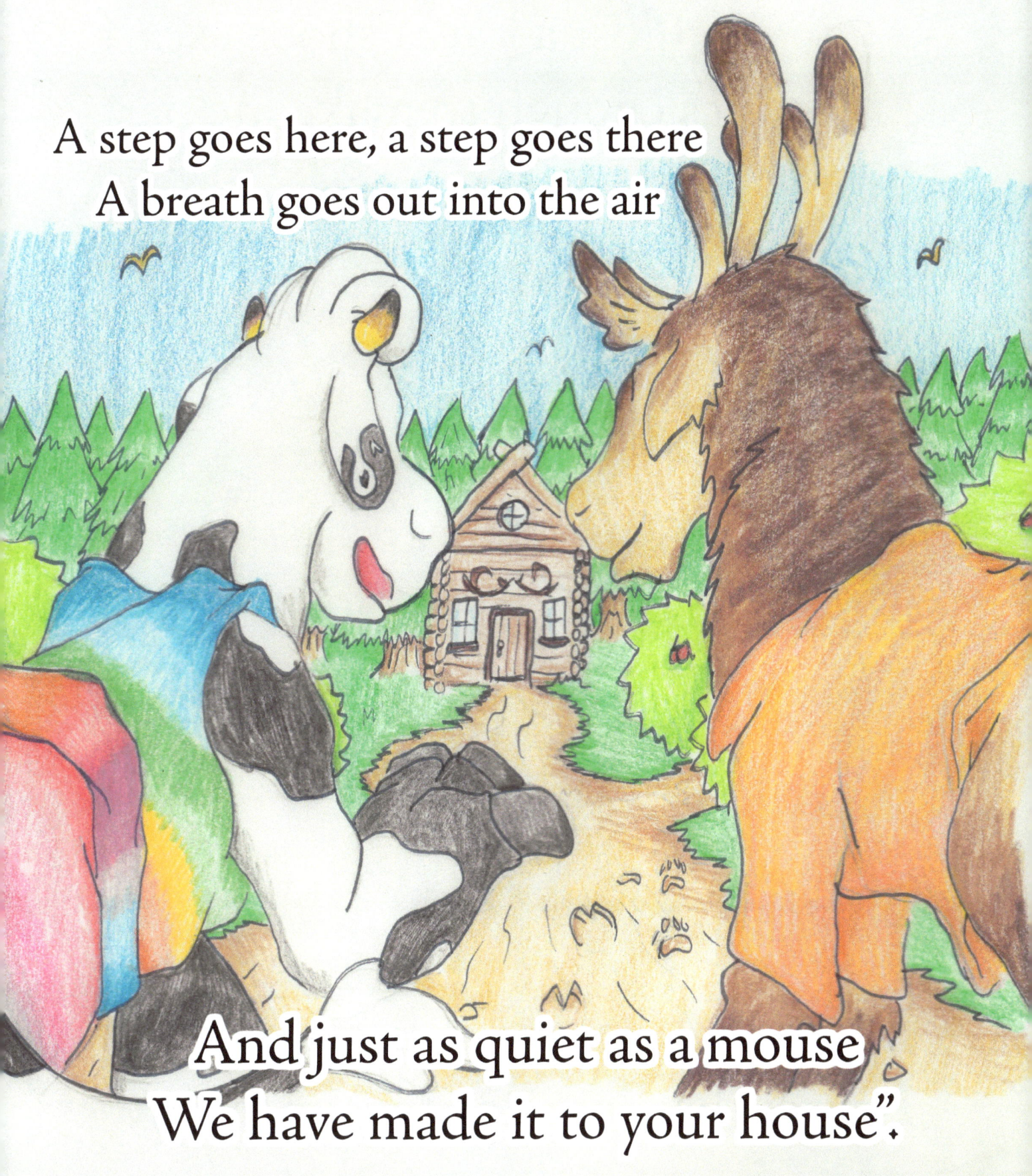

"And with each hoof-step forward go
Focus on your muscles so

A step goes here, a step goes there
A breath goes out into the air

And just as quiet as a mouse
We have made it to your house".

"Oh yes, I see that we are here
Where most of my things disappear
I lost a hat, a shoe, a scarf
It's enough to make me barf

All of my things run away
I guess they just don't want to stay"

"Well, we shall see" Now Cow said.
"I want to see your room, your bed

For if what I suspect is true
A simple task I'll set for you".

"Okay. Come in" the Caribou said
"Here's my room and here's my bed"

Now Cow walked in to quite a sight
It looked like there had been a fight

Among all the toys and clothes and stuff
It looked quite crazy and quite rough

Clothes were strewn from here to there
Toys were piled in the air
There was no room to sit or think
And something gave off quite a stink

It might have been a shoe or socks
It might have been the dirt and rocks
Where something green and fuzzy grew.
The room was messy through and through.

Now Cow breathed in and then breathed out.
"Caribou" she said, "I'd like to turn about

And walk my cow self far away
But you're a friend and so I'll stay".

"So here's the plan. Here's what we'll do.
We'll clear it out, each sock and shoe.

Just like we clear thoughts from our mind
We'll clear the room and what we find

May surprise both me and you
You pick up. I'll pick up too"

"Together we can make some space
To help you keep your room a place

Where peacefulness is always found
And chaos cannot stick around"

And so they worked side by side
Shaggy fur and spotted hide.

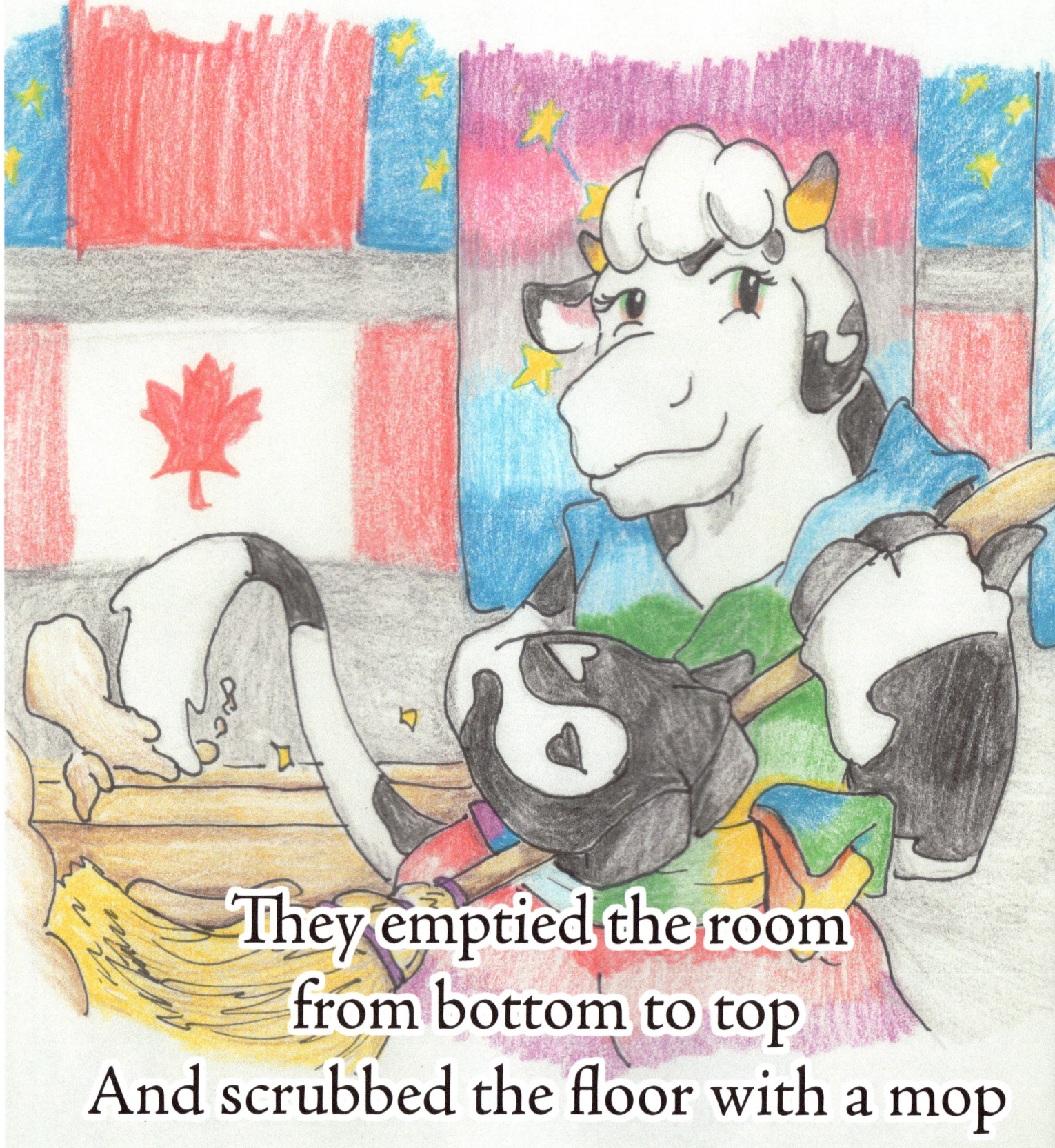

They emptied the room
from bottom to top
And scrubbed the floor with a mop

They cleaned the windows
and washed the walls
They even tidied
up the halls

And with everything clean and everything bare
Now Cow said, "Caribou, have a care
About the things you bring inside
For if it does not bring you pride

Maybe it should not come back
For you want to keep on track
Everything that you bring in
Should bring your heart and mind a win"

Caribou sat and thought
Something he had not done a lot

He wondered, "Does it bring me joy?
To have each jumbled cluttered toy?"

And though it was hard to part
He found he had a lighter heart

With smaller amounts
of trucks and things
Less chaos and more joy it brings

He cut his toys and junk by half
He shouted out with a laugh

"I'm keeping only 20 toys
And giving the rest to other boys

And other girls might like my books
Or cars or stuffed rhinoceros"

"And clothes too old and clothes too small
That I have gotten at the mall

I'll sell them or give them away
To those who can't afford to pay"

Now Cow nodded and approved
Of Caribou's more joyful mood

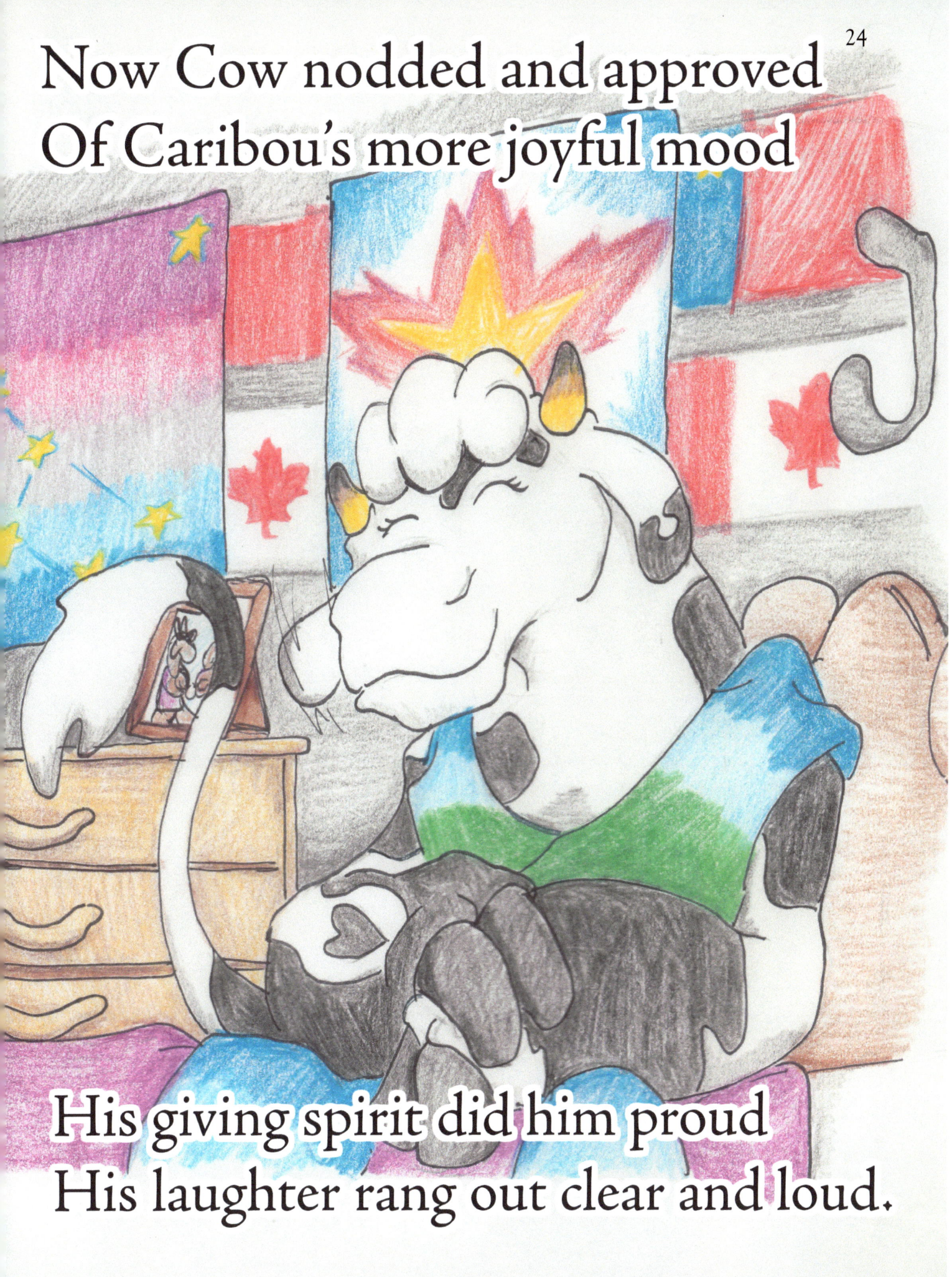

His giving spirit did him proud
His laughter rang out clear and loud.

But that's not all. There's more to say
For each and every other day

When Caribou put things away
He found that in their place they'd stay

And he lost no more of his stuff
And when he was tempted to huff

Or be upset
about his day
He thought on
things a peaceful way

And he did not have to wait
To keep his focus pointed straight.

For when he'd walk, he'd meditate.
Breathe in and hold. Count to eight.

And then breathe out slow and sure
To make his heart and mind more pure.

He and Now Cow stayed good friends.
And that is how this story ends.

CPSIA information can be obtained
at www.ICGtesting.com
Printed in the USA
LVHW011515121220
674006LV00001B/12